FIESOLE MUSEI

FIESOLE
Archaeological Site and Museum

Marco de Marco

GIUNTI

Index

Graphic design: Franco Bulletti
Translation: Ailsa Wood for Lexis, Florence
Drawings: Alessandro Bartolozzi
Archivio Fotografico Fiesole Musei

ISBN 88-09-01330-1

Introduction

This guide is divided into two parts: the first illustrates the archaeological site, three hectares of hilly countryside where the superb ruins of the ancient theatre, the baths and the Etruscan-Roman temple are located. The second offers an itinerary of the Museum, a journey across Fiesole's history through archaeological findings.

Our aim is to share with the public the absorbing experience that those of us who work and write here daily feel under our skin: the contact with a uniquely beautiful and gently harmonious site, rich in archaeological and historical heritage and intensely stimulating. Above all, a place that is unique and homogenous in all its elements, from the ruins of the ancient theatre to the short aromatic grass, from the hundred-year-old olive trees to the young plum trees, from the pairs of blackbirds to the many cats, from the splendid walnut trees to the stern cypresses. The intention is to preserve the whole without damaging any of its parts, and this is my task. If I may set a little task for those who visit us here, I'd like to ask you to visit the site and Museum calmly and attentively. Don't spare us your criticism if it is required! Above all, take part, and I hope that the experience of a day spent here will be positive and enriching for you all.

MARCO DE MARCO
Fiesole Museum Curator

3

The Archaeological Site

The Roman theatre

The excavations which brought to light the theatre took place in several stages throughout the 19th century. The Government Commission for Etruscan Antiquities undertook the excavations in 1870. Three years later the land forming the current archaeological site was purchased by the council, and in 1877 the Council Archaeological Commission was formed, under the direction of Demostene Macciò, who brought the building totally to light over a period of twenty years. The commission also undertook the restoration work but although there are no reconstruction errors or alterations in the left-hand side of the staircase, the same cannot be said for the vaulted rooms alongside the proscenium.

1. Roman theatre. Overall view.

2. Roman theatre. In the background: the belltower of San Romolo.

The central part of the *cavea* rested on the rocks of the hillside and the ends of each side were supported by vaulted constructions corresponding to the *parodoi* of the Greek theatre. These also provided access to the lower staircases, particularly the marble seats situated in the *orchestra* and reserved for important figures. Above these passages were the *tribunalia* arcades with other reserved seats. The staircases consisted of ten tiers of steps dissected by three small flights in four wedge-shapes: only the right-hand part is original and the steps are still preserved, made from large blocks placed one on top of the other and slightly cut into the rock following a typical

7

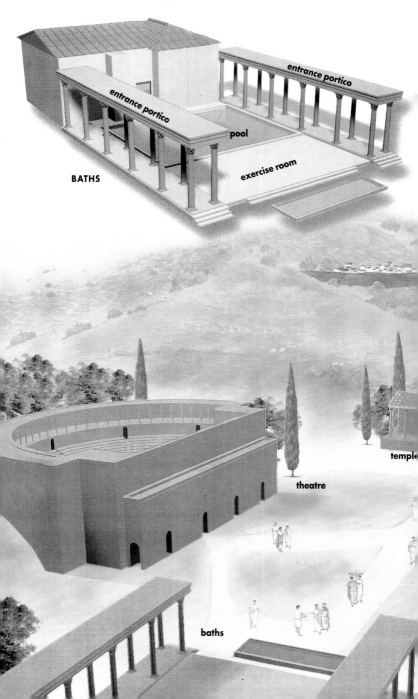

BATHS

entrance portico

entrance portico

pool

exercise room

theatre

temple

baths

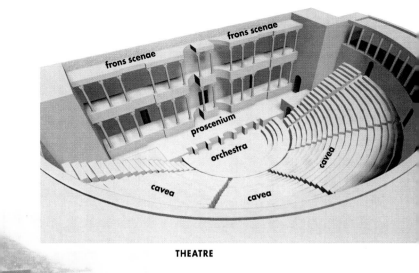

THEATRE

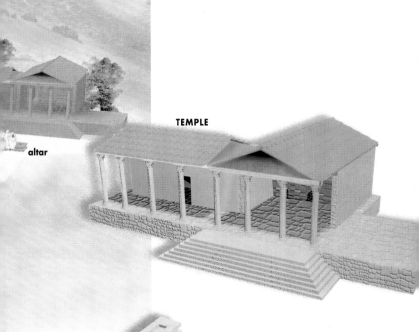

altar

TEMPLE

altar

3. View of archaeo-logical site from the theatre.

system found in the oldest theatres. The *cavea* leads to the *vomitoria*, with entrances made from four large slabs worn down only at the joint and positioned dry. These passageways were equipped with double doors - a hinge can still be seen in one of them - which were then closed with cross bars. As well as these entrances, two side staircases further facilitated the spectators' movement.

At the front of the *cavea* was the *orchestra* on whose floor the excavations revealed traces of a multicoloured mosaic. In the ancient Greek theatre this space was allotted to chorus movements but already in the Hellenistic era the action usually took place on the proscenium, restricted to the front by the wall of the *pulpitum* and at the rear by an architectural wall, the *frons scenae*, and to the sides by the *versurae*. From the eastern *versura*, across a vaulted passageway, the spectators in

4. Roman theatre. Overall view of proscenium.

the highest seats could move down into the portico behind the scena. Nothing remains of this portico except nine extensively restored stone pillars. From this same *versura* it was also possible to reach the *choragia*, the store-rooms where costumes and stage materials were kept.

Only the foundation of the *frons scenae* remains, which is however sufficient to show us the three doors used by actors to enter the stage: at the centre the *porta regia* and to the sides the *portae hospitales*. The semi-circular room behind the western *versura* would have been used for moving the curtain which folded back inside a groove. This is now underground but was once visible after the excavation, situated immediately behind the *pulpitum*.

The building is usually dated at the last quarter of the 1st century BC (the particular construction technique of the walls, with its

11

*5. Roman theatre.
Room for curtain
movement.*

small bossing elements, and the rounded central niche of the *frons scenae* can be seen). The building was to undergo decorative improvements between the end of the 2nd and the beginning of the 3rd century BC.

Further confirmation derives from an archaeological sample carried out in the upper part immediately behind the *cavea*, which provided material dating back to the end of the 1st century BC.

6. Roman street and shrine bases between the theatre and temple.

Near the theatre is perhaps the most important urban element: a wide street which has been dated at the Imperial period by recent sampling. The street led from the Forum square and formed one of the axes of the city plan, probably the *cardo*.

Close by, three rectangular stone bases can still be seen in step formation and partly covered in marble. It is not easy to interpret their function but it is supposed that they were the bases of commemorative monuments.

The Roman baths

Like the theatre, this building was also extensively restored when it was uncovered. The work took place simultaneously with the uncovering of the monument but hardly took into consideration the facts which gradually emerged. The complex is more or less completely visible but its architectural history is not known and can only be generally reconstructed through the construction techniques and few preserved elements of marble decoration.

The baths consisted of two parts: an interior, covered part for the hot baths and an outside part with two pools, the larger of which was for plunging. A room can be seen between the two pools, perhaps the *cryptoporticus*, and

7. Roman baths. Pool.

beside them on the northern and southern sides, were two long rectangular rooms which have been identified as the wings of a portico. On the northern side the walls were also low to allow space for a small arcade with a view over the Mugnone valley.

The covered section was divided into the usual three rooms: from south to north, the *calidarium* (with *opus signimum* floor supported by brick pillars through which the hot air passed to heat the room, and three small pools on the west, south and east sides); the *tepidarium*, a moderately heated through-room leading to the northernmost and oldest room, the *frigidarium*. This was subdivided by three arches, rebuilt with extensive use of modern elements, into two parts. The west side consisted of a large room with a niche which probably held a statue. The eastern side contained a semi-circular pool whose cover-

8. Roman baths. Cryptoportico.

15

9. Roman baths. Calidarium.

10. Roman baths. Detail of calidarium heating system.

11. Roman baths. Ovens for heating calidarium.

ing and bottom have been totally lost. The lavatories can still be seen behind this room.

The warm part of the building was served by three ovens, two situated behind the *calidarium* and one behind the *tepidarium*.

The particular location of the baths, especially on the southern and eastern sides, favoured their subsequent burial as the terracing work carried out at the time of construction gradually gave way. It is not possible to establish when the bath buildings ceased to be used but the restoration work carried out during the 3rd century is an indication, as in the other preserved monumental buildings, of the city's last period of well-being before the crisis of the 5th century.

The Etruscan-Roman temple

The temple is situated at the northern end of the archaeological site. Its position in the ancient period is still unclear: some of the buildings uncovered in particular have a different orientation to the later ones, perhaps belonging to a small place of worship. As far as we know the construction of the Etruscan temple at the close of the 4th century BC represented the first systematic organisation of the area, perhaps connected to the construction of the walls.

When it was built the land was levelled by extensive earthing-up and chiselling of the rocks. The filling earth was piled up in fairly regular layers, the last of which formed the floor surface on the *pronaos* and the *alae*. The foundations were placed on the rock following the height differences, while in the rear part of the building a deep trench was made to allow the water from the hill above to drain away in two small gutters running along the side foundations of the temple.

The fortuitous preservation of a large part of the walls of the facade allows us to reconstruct the plan of the building, which was rectangular with a single central cella and two *antae* coinciding with the external line of the stylobate. Between the two *antae* there must have been columns but no trace of them is visible. There was certainly no second row of columns: the front part, the *pars antica*, was completely empty and alone took up almost

12. Etruscan temple. View.

half the total length of the building. A step led up to the cella: the floor was about 20cm higher than the *pronaos*. The position in which most of the antefixes were found confirms that the roof also covered the *alae* without extending too far over the side wall. However no information is available about the slope of the two pitches, the roof of the front section or the features of the pediment.

In front of the steps up to the temple was an altar with ovolo frame, now visible at a higher level than its original one.

The destruction of the temple and the construction of another on the same place, with the same plan, but typically Roman monumental dimensions, marked the end of the Etruscan town's independence and the beginning of its "Romanisation".

A new plan was created, the Etruscan staircase was covered and the altar in front of it, and a new access staircase was built (on the

13. Roman temple. View of staircase and large shrine in front.

outside) framed above by two monumental shaped podiums. Much larger blocks of stone were used in the construction than those used in the Etruscan temple. Not far from the Etruscan altar, and on the same line, is the large Roman altar, which was also buried during the last rearrangement of the site in the 3rd century, with later raising of the floor level, bringing the difference in height between the Etruscan level of the 4th century BC and the Roman one in the 3rd century AD to about 4m. The temple fell into disuse, probably during the 5th century and during the 6th-7th centuries AD a Longobard burial ground was placed there, of which remains have been found all over the archaeological site.

The Longobard tombs in the archaeological site

The excavation of part of the Longobard burial ground near the Etruscan-Roman temple was carried out by Edoardo Galli, supervisor of the Etruscan Antiquities Service between 1910 and 1912. The tombs covered the whole area of the building with higher concentration in the space corresponding to the old cella, and its structure must still have been visible when the cemetery foundations were laid.

14. Longobard tomb situated between the ruins of the "cella" of the Etruscan temple. 6th-7th centuries AD.

However, we know that other tombs were discovered during the excavations of the baths - one is still visible near the so-called *cryptoporticus* - and legend claims the discovery in the early 19th century of two tombs rich in con-

tents the upper area of the theatre. Moreover, during the excavations after 1910, especially between 1927 and 1930, other tombs were seen in the area including the theatre and the temple.

The tombs were all simply built with dry stone or slab walls and coverings made of large stone slabs, following the construction model of the late Ancient period and Middle Ages. Some of these also had stone floors. It was also noted that materials from old Etruscan and Roman buildings were often re-used, and that, at least in the temple area, the tombs were arranged in irregular rows all facing east-west. Judging by the accessories three of the tombs are certainly men's and five women's: the others are difficult to identify. Thanks to a type of clasp discovered, it can be established that the cemetery was used from the end of the 6th century AD and throughout the 7th. In the whole burial ground area only one weapon was found, the point of a lance in tomb 4 dating back to the second half of the 7th century.

The surrounding walls

The city's precise position is still evident, reinforced by a surrounding wall about 2.5km long. It is still too complicated to date the construction and any narrowing, widening and other modifications carried out on the wall over time. Gallic incursions in the 4th century certainly played a part in the erection of walls to defend the Etruscan cities, but the possibility that a circle of walls, perhaps smaller, or the construction of some parts, may even have existed much earlier cannot be completely ruled out. Some excavation samples taken immediately under the inside of the north side walls seem to show

15. Section of Etruscan walls on the San Francesco hill. 4th-3rd centuries BC.

16. Section of Etruscan walls on southern slope. 4th-3rd centuries BC.

that at least in that area they were closely connected to the rearrangement of the site that took place under the Romans. When the city came under Roman rule and lost, for a long time, any strategic importance, the old Etruscan walls were not destroyed but mainly used in the new urban system which required more solid buildings than the previous ones. In subsequent periods there is even less evidence available.

We know from Procopius of Caesarea that Fiesole was known for its walls and fortifications and was contested at length between 539 and 542, during the war between the Goths and the Byzantines. The walls were therefore still standing at that time and they remained throughout the Middle Ages: in 1125 they were the greatest obstacle to the Florentines in their conquest of Fiesole. The demolition of the walls was decreed and due their sheer size their construction was attributed to mythological Giants.

A first section of wall, about 250m long, is to be found immediately below the archaeological site, on the northern side of the city. On the western side outlets of two large basins collecting the water from above the city can be seen, and even higher, the probable remains of a gate. Near the baths the bases of five stone pillars have been preserved, which belonged to a small arcade situated behind the walls in Roman times. The walls are then buried under today's streets and houses and their route, running from here up to the Borgunto hill, can only be imagined, with the help of extensively rearranged small segments, preserved in the private gardens and allotments. However the walls led up the slope to the south-east excluding the via del Bargellino burial ground. On the Borgunto hill another section of the walls is visible, about 180m long and 4m high. The walls continue under Sant'Appollinare, a small church of ancient origins, and then turn south. Near the corner of via di Montececeri and via di Doccia they led down to via Fra' Giovanni Angelico where a long section rises above the street along the entrance road to villa "Il Roseto". Another section of the walls can be seen at the convent of San Girolamo, but it is rather different from the others, perhaps because it was built in a different period or by different builders, or perhaps it is not part of the real circle of walls but one of its terracing walls. Other sections of wall can be seen on the San Francesco hill but it is unlikely that they are only fortifications because a part of them could have formed the system of terracing with which the steep slope of the hill was shaped.

17. Section of Etruscan walls on the Sant'Apollinare hill. 4th-3rd centuries BC.

The local sandstone was used for the construction of the walls and also most of the public and private buildings, particularly the grey and *serena* types typical of the Fiesole hills.

It is not easy to trace a particular quarry but considering the sheer bulk of the blocks of stone and the resulting problems involved in transporting them, it is reasonable to suppose that the materials came either from the very place the walls were built or from quarries located close by.

The via Bargellino tombs

In the area between via del Bargellino and via Matteotti, between the end of the 19th and the middle of the 20th centuries, six chamber tombs were found from the Etruscan Hellenistic period (3rd century BC). Two of these can still be seen today.

These are the only tombs in Fiesole about which something is known, and they belong to one of the Hellenistic burial grounds situated immediately outside the walls. They were extensively reused during Imperial Roman times and in some even late Ancient period graves were found. The tombs were situated along

18. Remains of Etruscan tombs in via del Bargellino.

one of the access roads to the city and were arranged to accommodate the slope of the rock, which at that point descends steeply from south to north.

The structure of the tombs is identical except in a few unimportant details: a rectangular room built from large blocks of *pietra serena* stone placed dry on top of each other, the interior space used to its fullest capacity with the construction of platforms with several steps on the side and end walls. Placed on these were urns, parallelepiped boxes with a flat or double pitch lid. The accessories (displayed inside the museum) were quite simple and included small terracotta balsam containers and in one case, a small bronze spatula. The most recent additions are represented by egg-shaped urns with lid and concave handle which can be dated within the first half of the 1st century AD. The most customary funeral rite was cremation, but the later graves are indicated by buried corpses.

Among the most interesting items discovered in these tombs are: a fragment of a small *pietra serena* urn with a Volterra-style illustrated box dating back to the 2nd century BC; an egg-shaped terracotta urn with flattened conical lid from the end of the 1st century BC; a fragment of a lamp disc with illustration of Aesculapius from the late Republican age.

The Museum:
its History and Collections

The Museum: its History and Collections

Ground floor: Fiesole and surrounding area

Room I ▶ Protohistorical, Etruscan and Roman materials from the town centre. Etruscan bronzes and burial stones ("stele fiesolane").

Room II ▶ Items from Etruscan and Roman burial grounds. Findings from the area. Roman burial stones. Lead containers from the Roman age.

Room III ▶ The archaeological site: theatre, baths, temple. Architectural decorations and materials. Temporarily on display, while awaiting permanent location, the bronze "she-wolf" from the 2nd century BC.

Room IV ▶ Materials from archaeological site. Marble slabs from the altars: scene of victory after a naval battle.

Room V ▶ Reconstruction of a Longobard tomb.

Room VI ▶ Archaeological research status, documents concerning the city and surrounding area.

Room VII ▶ Late Ancient period (4th-5th centuries).

Room VIII ▶ Longobard and early Middle Ages (6th - 8th centuries).

First floor: Collections

Room IX-X ▶ Costantini Collection

Room XI ▶ Strozzi Collection and various

Room XII ▶ Colombaria Collection and various

Room XII-XIII ▶ Albites Collection

F

iesole Archaeological Museum, which is currently being rearranged, aims to record the city's history, from the first settlements on the hills overlooking the Arno plain up until the development of the Etruscan and Roman civilisations, the "Barbaric" invasions, the arrival of the Longobards and the slow rising of the medieval city. When the fitting work is complete, the visitors' route will be chronological, with objects displayed to their best advantage as documentary items while respecting their differing origins.

Since the very beginning, the Museum has been a centre both for the collection and documentation of items being discovered in various circumstances in Fiesole and its surroundings, and those arriving from different sources. These items usually come from private collections belonging to residents or those who took part in public life in Fiesole or in the local and regional archaeological research in the late 19th and early 20th centuries. Some of these were responsible for bringing to light Fiesole's most important Etruscan and Roman monuments: the Marchese Carlo Strozzi, for example, took part personally at his own expense in the excavation of the theatre.

More recently the traditional donation of objects and archaeological findings to the Museum has been revived with the donation of Professor Costantini's own collection of pottery from Greece, Graecia Magna and Etruria.

The Museum thus consists of two sections, which, in its current organisation, are also physically separate: the topographical section occupies the ground floor and the collections are displayed on the first floor.

While we await the overall rearrangement of the Museum, which will begin with the re-organisation of the early Medieval and Medieval room, the Fiesole material remains organised in a strictly topographical manner, that is, divided according to area of origin. This makes available precise analytical material regarding the wealth and problems of the city's archaeological site but makes it more difficult for the visitor to grasp the fundamental elements of the results of archaeological research in Fiesole. This small guide aims to prefigure what will be the historical-chronological route, highlighting some representative objects for each period in the various rooms of the Museum and accompanying them with brief notes on the city's ancient history.

Fiesole
before Fiesole

After sporadically documented settlements from the 2nd millennium BC, it became possible from the 10th-9th centuries to follow the organisation of a settlement of increasing importance, especially due to its favourable position overlooking the Arno plain near the Appennine passes.

It can be supposed that distinct groups of

19. Two fragments of household pottery with carved geometric decoration. Mid-Bronze Age.

20. Half of fusion sandstone tablet. Mid-Bronze Age.

21. Fragment of funeral urn with geometric graffiti decorations. Villanovan civilisation. 10th-8th century BC.

huts were present on the hill, probably on the high ground overlooking the central saddle and linked from east-west and from north-south by a network of roads which crossed the hill and determined the organisation of the settlement.

Around the inhabited areas were burial grounds which have never been found.

type of fusion

point

(hill now location of San Francesco convent)

groups of huts with woven reed walls and straw and clay rooves

Fiesole in the ancient period (7th - 6th century BC)

Although for the moment we have little information, it can be assumed that already in the 6th century complex urban organisation was already taking place, with the presence of fairly large buildings. We know in particular that two temples existed on the two opposite slopes, to the north and south: these have yielded a series of fragments which can partly be traced back to pottery votive objects, and two votive offerings consisting of small bronze male and female figures offering worship. The votive offering from the temple on the southern slope, which came to light accidentally and was recovered, and is known to the archaeological bibliography as "the Villa Marchi votive offering", consisted of about forty bronze figures, both male and fe-

22-24. Small bronze votive offering statues from Villa Marchi, with left hand turned down to evoke underground deities and the right hand holding a pomegranate, symbol of immortality. 5th century BC.

male. The figures are shown in the ritual position of evocation of underground deities, with the left hand turned downwards with the palm open and a pomegranate, the symbol of immortality, held in the right hand.

In these votive offerings the original trapeziform stone bases for the statues were discovered. These were placed by the priest in special wooden offerings inside the temple. Once they were full, they were emptied, the bronzes removed and placed in special holes dug below the floor of the cella (the most holy room of the temple where the statue of the deity was kept and which could only be entered by the priest). For an archaeologist it is therefore a great stroke of luck to come across one of these holes: this is exactly what happened in 1931 to Mingazzini who brought to light this example.

The votive offering from the temple on the northern slope yielded rather less; the temple was located in the same area where the Etruscan temple and later the Roman one would be rebuilt (note that inside the ruins of the Ro-

25. Fragment of multi-coloured antefix. 6th-5th centuries BC.

man temple a small church emerged, probably in Longobard times, confirming the continued use of the location for religious worship). The fragments of the multicoloured antefix depicting the head of Medusa belong to the older temple.

We have no way of knowing on the other hand whether the inhabited area was already encircled by walls, and we can only imagine, by comparisons with contemporary settlements, the features of the dwellings.

However we do possess a great deal of material from this period, especially clay mix and red earth pottery which represent a high quality of production discovered in various parts of the area, indicative of the organisation and growth of commerce.

A typical item produced in Fiesole and its surroundings in that time is the *pietra serena* burial stone, known as "pietre fiesolane" (stones of Fiesole).

Fiesole cannot be considered to be the only centre manufacturing this typical product, which as well as burial stones included a series of boundary stones of various shapes and sizes. The most imposing of these is the "cippo di Settimello" now preserved in the Archaeological Museum in Florence. Considering the in loco availability of *pietra serena*, there must have been very highly skilled craftsmen in Fiesole, who were also perhaps itinerant artists.

The original location of the burial stones and boundary posts is still, in some ways, under discussion. They were probably situated on the summit or inside the large family bur-

26. Fiesolano burial stone from Travignoli (Pontassieve). 6th-5th centuries BC. The three panels show scenes from burials and ceremonies in honour of the dead; the funeral banquet, the procession accompanied by flute-players, animals fighting.

ial mounds which characterised the burial sites of the farming and merchant aristocracy in this part of Etruria in the 7th and 6th centuries..

The Museum storerooms contain other fragments of ancient Etruscan monuments in Fiesole *pietra serena* which will soon be displayed.

The life and development of a northern Etruscan city (5th-2nd century BC)

For Fiesole (whose Etruscan name was probably VIPSL), the classical age and Hellenism represented a period of intense development and increase in economical and social well-being. Contacts, relations and exchanges with other Etruscan towns increased, particularly with Volterra and Chiusi to the south and the towns on and beyond the Apennines to the north. This led to urban development, with the gradual foundation of a single centre which was eventually to cover the high grounds to the east and west. During the 4th century, at the time of the Gallic incursions, the inhabited area was surrounded

27. Buildings between via Marini and via Portigiani.

28. Boundary stone (museum portico). 4th century BC.

by a powerful circle of walls about 2.5 kilometres long, probably modelled on an older one.

The imposing terracing walls were to become a fundamental element of the new urban organisation during the 4th-3rd centuries. They stretched longitudinally along the slope from east to west, and gave the town a char-

29. Etruscan temple. 4th-3rd centuries BC.

hill currently occupied convent of San Franc

TEMPLE

service rooms

cella

entrance staircase

service rooms

altar

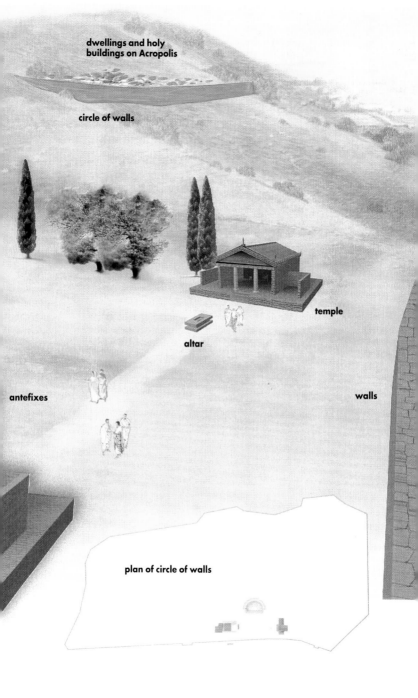

dwellings and holy
buildings on Acropolis

circle of walls

temple

altar

antefixes

walls

plan of circle of walls

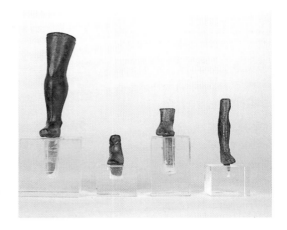

30. Votive offerings.
4th-3rd centuries
BC.

acteristic terraced appearance, linked by roads
and flights of steps, and easily seen from a dis-
tance. Some of these walls can be seen from
the Museum.

The extensive area under the influence of
the town, and from which it drew its wealth,
particularly in farming terms (the Roman his-
torian Livy also records the fertility of "Etruscan fields"), bordered to the south with
Volterra and Arezzo and to the north with what
is now Mugello and the Appennines. A public
boundary post is displayed in the Museum
which concerns the territory and people of
Fiesole.

The extreme care taken with marking public and private property limits in Etruscan
times is underlined by another small stone
post displayed in the first room. With the ex-
ception of the terraces, the only Etruscan-Hel-
lenistic period building entirely visible today
is the temple.

The materials discovered during the exca-

31. Attic terracotta head antefix. 4th-3rd centuries BC.

32. Terracotta element from pediment, perhaps part of a scene depicting the fight between brothers Eteocles and Polynices under the walls of Thebes. 3rd-2nd centuries BC.

vations of the building include remains of the original architectural decorations and of the votive offerings, consisting mainly of small bronzes showing the parts of the body for which the deity's healing powers were invoked. This deity has been identified as Minerva due to the discovery of a small bronze owl.

One of the most interesting pieces in the Museum, dating back to the late Hellenistic period, is the powerful bronze torso of an animal which was for a long time identified as a she-wolf, but was subsequently recognised, although with some reserve, as a lioness. This torso would have been part of a group which perhaps included the depiction of the Lady of the Animals, placed on the top of or near to an important public building. The piece was discovered in Fiesole in 1882 near the monumental remains of a late Hellenistic building near what is now piazza Garibaldi (part of these buildings, which are in some way linked to those discovered near via Marini, are still visible in the garden of Palazzo Mangani). Due to a series of findings including a small Roman marble post with an inscription concerning restoration work, these ruins are thought to belong to the Campidoglio of Roman Fiesole. This was the source for the identification of the beast's torso as a "she-wolf" and its dating at the 1st century BC. But more recently, especially due to the anatomical features, the animal has been recognised as a lioness, although some elements of doubt remain, especially owing to the incongruence of the undoubtedly female sexual features and the mane which would seem a more masculine characteristic. The

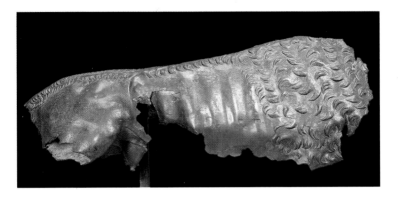

33. Bronze torso of lioness. 2nd-1st century BC.

dating too has undergone modifications: to-day it is generally believed that the so-called "*lupa*" can be dated at least to the 2nd century BC and may be one element of a group of statues, which perhaps included a lion, on a large Hellenistic public building.

The piece is made from a cast carried out using the indirect "cire perdue" method in a single casting. The superficial casting defects have been obscured by rectangular or square dowelling. The treatment of the fur in relief is embellished with cold-work retouching carried out using an outlining chisel, as well as some tiny relief hemispheres. The alloy is a ternary type (copper 83-84%, tin 11-12%, lead 4-5%). The features of this sculpture have lead to its dating between the 2nd and 1st centuries BC.

Roman Fiesole (1st century BC - 5th century AD)

At the end of the 2nd century BC and the beginning of the 1st, many other cities in Etruria experienced the radicalization of their encounter with Rome, which increased its strength to the north and, in a quest for new lands to redistribute among its campaigners, battled with the farming aristocracy in northern Etruscan cities. This too was Fiesole's fate.

In the year 90 BC, the town was conquered by Roman troops under the command of the consul Porcius Cato. It was a violent conquest and the fires spread through the city destroying buildings and leaving traces in the layers and structures of the Etruscan temple. The stratigraphy in particular seems to underline the fact that the building was not immediately rebuilt but indeed that the area was completely abandoned for a brief period after the fires. This was probably true of the whole of Fiesole. This then was the traumatic beginning of the "Romanisation" of a city still permeated with Etruscan culture and traditions (the tradition handed down by Silius Italicus recalls it as famous among Etruscan cities for its school of interpretation of lightning, one of the branches of the "Etruscan discipline").

The construction began of typical buildings such as the theatre and the baths, as well as the reconstruction of the temple, and in the city and surroundings typically Roman objects and products became diffused. Objects from this

34. Stone burial epigraph mentioning priests of Saturn.
1st century AD.

35. Stone burial epigraph mentioning dendrophori corporation.
1st century AD.

period can be seen in the 2nd and 3rd rooms of the Museum. In room 2, next to the accessories from the last Etruscan tombs (which can still be seen in via del Bargellino), are epigraphs from the burial grounds arranged around the city.

From some of these we have learned of the existence in Fiesole of religious and crafts corporations like for example the *dendrophori* of Attys or the priests of Saturn.

*36. Head of male
togaed figure.
1st century AD.*

*37. Marble slab.
1st century AD.*

The best recorded building, especially due to its state of preservation and the quantity of materials it has yielded (compared, for example, to the baths) is undoubtedly the theatre.

Of the particularly valuable marble decorations many fragments remain of illustrated slabs which decorated the wall of the proscenium and the *frons scenae*. These are decorated with purely ornamental motifs mainly representing plants but also illustrated mythical scenes and deities: in one we can clearly

38. Marble slab showing naval victory.
1st century AD.

recognise Dionysus, the god connected with the origins of the theatre, leaning on a herm and accompanied by a panther. A stylistic analysis of the slabs revealed a restoration of the building's decorations around the 3rd century AD.

During the excavation many fragments of pottery deposited in the temple were discovered inside the filling earth which gradually covered the building. Quite a large number of terracotta lamps were also discovered dating back to between the 1st and 2nd centuries AD. The figure depicted like the emperor Claudius, in a marble statue, of which only the head remains, was perhaps connected with the construction of the building.

39. Statues of Isis and Osiris dedicated to Gargennio Macrino of Fiesole. 2nd century AD.

Another head was found which instead probably represents Messalina rather than a prominent figure from Fiesole.

Material from the baths is extremely scarce and worth mentioning are only the fragments of bronze sheets with epigraphs and the marble base belonging to a statue of Hercules which decorated the wall opposite the *frigidarium* pool. Other items illustrating habits and customs in Roman Fiesole are present in the Museum. As well as the household and table pottery, other special and typical items include the statues of Isis and Osiris, which indicate the penetration of oriental worship into the city, on the return of the campaigners from the wars in the Orient, and the large lead cist with relief decorations.

40. Lead cist. Container for solid matter, perhaps grain, linked to an Imperial donation. 2nd-3rd century AD.

The crisis period (5th-6th century AD)

After a series of restorations which can be dated at around the 3rd century, (documented in all the important monumental buildings especially the theatre and the baths, from the second half of the 4th century AD and increasingly clearly in the 5th century) some areas previously inhabited and then transformed into cemeteries were clearly abandoned.

Other areas were transformed and at the same time the buildings impoverished: for example, rooms were subdivided or given a different orientation compared to the previous period. Therefore a restriction of the inhabited areas and change in their function must have occurred, rather than a common phenomenon throughout the city. However for most of the 5th century manufacturing levels and quality do not seem to have been impoverished in terms of materials used and production diffusion.

High quality materials were still circulating (for example, glass or certain pottery tableware discovered in the via Marini excavations) which prove that the city was commercially active and in contact, through a largely practicable road network of Roman construction, with economically active surrounding area. Nor can we ignore the presence of tombs in areas previously occupied by Roman buildings, proof that the previous urban situation was suffering and its transformation was about to begin.

Fiesole in the Greek-Gothic war (539-542)

Frolom the text of Procopius of Caesarea who narrates the war between the Goths and the Byzantines for the possession of Italy, we know that Fiesole was contested at length and fell under the rule of each between 539 and 542.

These war years considerably weakened the town, which, despite some signs of crisis in the previous century, had in some way "held on" during the 5th century. The favourable aspects of Fiesole's dominant and strategic position in the area is clear from these events and it was an easier bastion to defend than to

41. View of Museum interior. The section devoted to the late Ancient and early Medieval periods begins here. In the foreground, the Longobard tomb discovered in the area behind today's Council building.

conquer, especially due to the gigantic Etruscan walls. Stories and legends began to develop around the walls, attributing their construction to Giants, and these continued, and were gradually embellished with fantastic elements, up until the Renaissance. Evidence of the Goth and Byzantine presence in Fiesole is to be found in the tradition, probably later, of the defeat of the Goth army in the area and the presence in the town of King Radagasio and his wife Agabita. We also know that the Gothic troops were starved out and the Byzantine garrison took their place.

42. Gothic earrings with polyhedral head, from Chianti. 6th century AD.

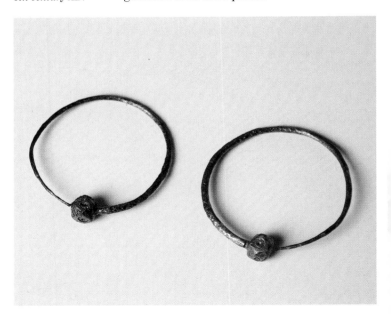

Fiesole in the Longobard age (6th-8th century)

43. Longobard tomb reconstructed inside archaeological museum. 6th-7th centuries AD.

When the Longobards arrived in Fiesole towards the end of the 6th century they found an extremely impoverished city and in the early part of their "occupation", the urban area was further narrowed down, to the extent that the burial grounds of that period occupied areas which in the Hellenistic and Roman periods were urbanised, although ancient grave sites.

partially ruined
stronghold walls

Ruins of theatre partially
buried

ruins of baths

longobard tombs
in the temple area

ruined temple buildings

ngobard tomb with
abs reused from Roman
ildings

44. *"Bottle" with painted decoration. Burial furnishing from Longobard period. 7th century AD.*

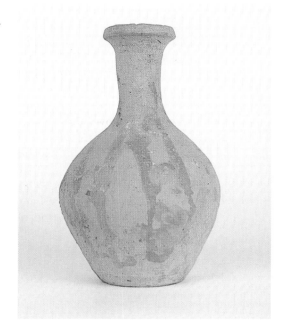

45. *Small "terra sigillata" jug and bowl of African manufacture. Burial furnishing from Longobard period. 7th century AD.*

The northern slope, occupied in Roman times by the theatre, baths, temple, streets and monumental altars, became a cemetery where a small place of worship may have been situated among the ruins of the Roman temple. In other parts of the city too it can be seen how the ancient Roman urban network, itself superimposed over the Hellenistic one, was overturned.

The population was organised into nuclei of various sizes arranged around places of worship or inside the old public buildings.

These must have been groups which, at least in the early period, placed themselves at random inside the old city, still mainly enclosed by the circle of walls, and the most important monumental aspect of the settlement, the single indication of a lost urban identity.

46. Small coloured paste necklace with central pendant made from perforated coin. Justinian era. Burial furnishing from Longobard period. 6th-7th century AD.

The Collections

The gallery section contains all the items donated at various times to the Museum.

As well as the Costantini Collection, the most recent donation (1986), one of the most outstanding is the collection of the Marchese Albites di San Paterniano who donated at various points between 1885 and 1922 archaeological items including Greek, Etruscan and Southern Italian pottery, sculptures and portraits from Imperial Rome and Roman and Etruscan funeral urns.

The Società Colombaria also donated materials to the Museum, mainly Etruscan red earth items from the excavations in the Chiusi and Sovana areas. Another memorable donor was Marchese Carlo Strozzi, a prominent figure in Florentine and Fiesolano archaeology at the end of the 19th century, who donated objects from various sources. Among these are the outstanding group of coins from the small treasury discovered in 1829. There have been many small donations, especially from local figures and administrators who thus intended to increase their own prestige and importance in the restricted local environment. This, basically was the archaeology of the period: passion, learning and detachment from everyday life. The Museum is a "shrine to antiquity", which only a few can enjoy. Thus, while in these years large building projects knocked down and completely destroyed the important archaeological remains in the whole of Fiesole, these same figures quietly continued to be "donors": objects from ancient Apulia, Lazio, Greece and Etruria entered the Museum leaving less and less space to the few preserved "fragments" from Fiesole. When the exploratory campaigns in the archaeological site begun by the then Etruscan Antiquity Service in the Thirties (and later with the beginning of the extensive excavations in the area of the Etruscan-Roman temple) were taken up again, the reassessment of the Museum's topographical aspect, which had already been conceived by the Head of the Service Milani and the Supervisor Galli. With the new arrangement, we aim to fulfil this basic concept of the Museum as a museum belonging to the city and its history. In this context, visiting the Museum's collections is first and foremost a way to experience today an archaeological form which has largely been left behind, but has not entirely disappeared, and was above all a quest for cultural standing and amateur passion.

The Costantini Collection

T he Fiesole Museum acquired the Collection in 1985 after Professor Alfiero Costantini donated the outstanding group of ceramics from Greece, Graecia Magna and Etruria that he had collected over many years, purchasing them primarily from antiques markets such as the Sotheby auctions, in Switzerland, the Antiques Exhibition in Florence and the art market in Milan.

The Museum was thus enriched by an important group of high quality ceramics, unfortunately with no information of their origins, from the main manufacturing areas of the ancient Mediterranean world between the 6th and 3rd centuries BC.

47. Perfumed oil containers, in shape of lying deer. Removable head acted as stopper. 7th century BC.

*48. Long
"alabastron"
(container for
perfumed oils
or unguents)
decorated with
animal friezes.
7th century BC.*

♦ *Corinthian pottery*

This type of product, which takes its name from the city of Corinth, was widespread in the whole Mediterranean area from Syria to Italy during the 7th and 6th centuries. Initially its typical range of shapes and decorations was neither extensive nor very varied, but was sophisticated, with motifs showing friezes of animals either isolated or in series on items linked to wine consumption (goblets, cups and jugs) or containers for perfume oils. From the end of the 7th century and in the first half of the 6th there was a decrease in production and in decorative motifs. After the mid-6th century, pottery production underwent a severe decline and standardisation, to the advantage of the Attic variety which from then on made its mark on all the Mediterranean markets.

♦ *Attic pottery with black figures*

This type of production began to distinguish itself from those in the surrounding areas during the 8th century, especially due to the desire to leave behind the geometric models characterising other products of the period, enlarging the space dedicated to illustrated items and narrative scenes.

In the 7th century bulky black figures began to appear with complex decorative scenes linked to the illustration of Homer's poems, with a wide use of graffito and clear imitation of the Corinthian pottery items which still dominated especially in terms of decorative motifs.

65

49. Black figure amphora with scenes of heroes fighting in the presence of Athena. 6th century BC.

50. Detail of decorations form a black figure amphora showing a warrior putting on armour. 6th century BC.

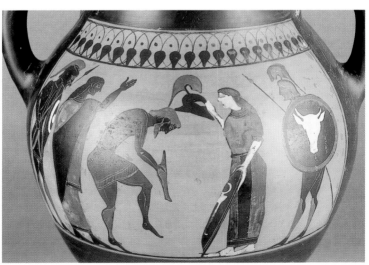

51. Black figure amphora depicting the capture of the dog Cerberus in Hades, one of the labours imposed on Hercules by Eurystheus. 6th century BC.

During the 6th century the success of Attic pottery over the Corinthian variety became increasingly clearer, and certain original personalities began to stand out, real "masters" of painting whose names are preserved on the pots: Amasis, Lydos, Exechias.

A less complex type of product (but still high quality although more serialised) was the so-called "miniaturist style", especially on long-stemmed goblets.

In the last thirty years of the 6th century experimentation began in the red figures style, which immediately after became widely diffused.

Black figure production continued however, also at high levels, (for example with Antimenes) but with the onset of the 5th century it became confined to commonly used objects, for example the Panathenaen amphorae and the burial *lekythoi*.

♦ *Attic pottery with red figures*

The characteristic feature of this variety is the black paint, used to fill in the illustrations, which is now spread all over the sides of the pots, apart from the figures and the decorations.

The details of the figures are painted in with a fine brush, with evident progress made in colour depiction. Among the first masters to use this technique without initially abandoning the black paint technique, were Euphro-

52. Large Attic production red figure "kylix". On the outside of the bowl are groups of musicians. 5th century BC.

nios, Euthymides, Oltos and Epiktetos, while in the early decades of the 5th century the painter Kleophrades and the Berlin painter were at work.

53. Large red figure "stamnos". The scene shows Poseidon's abduction of the beautiful Amymone. 5th century BC.

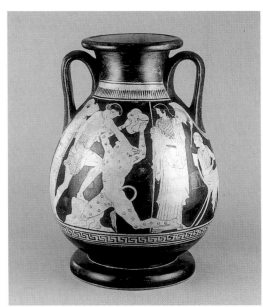

54. Red figure "pelike". Ariadne helps Theseus find his way though the labyrinth to kill the Minotaur. 5th century BC.

69

High quantitative and qualitative levels of production were achieved in the Periclean age with "masters" like the Polignoto Painter and the Kodros painter, an illustrator of mythical scenes connected to the Athenian myths.

In the last quarter of the 5th century after the great plague and the Peloponnesian war, there was a renewal of the rich and abundant decorative style of painting with a widespread use of the myth of Dionysus and Aphrodite, or funeral scenes.

Outstanding among the masters of this period was the Meidias painter.

After the conquest of Athens by Peloponnesos, Attic production market was greatly decreased along with its possibilities of diffusion.

In Athens the end of red figure production can be dated at the end of the 4th century, when the city entered the sphere of Macedonian culture.

55. Two-handled cup ("kantharos") with relief decoration. Italic household pottery. The shape derives from more valuable metal prototypes. 7th-6th centuries BC.

◆ *Clay mix pottery*

This type of production was mainly devoted to pots for daily use, and was made from unpurified clay, rich in additives.

The forms were shaped by hand in the more ancient periods, and subsequently on the wheel with more refined clay, and sometimes also painted with motifs from the Hellenistic range.

◆ *Etruscan black figure pottery*

Etruria constituted an important market for the production of Greek black figure pottery, thanks also to the presence of masters from

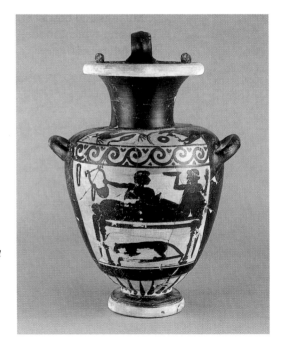

56. Water or other liquid container ("hydria") produced in Etruria in imitation of Greek black figure pots. At the centre is a banquet scene. 5th century BC.

Greece and Asia Minor after the Persian occupation halfway though the 6th century. From this time onwards black figure Etruscan production began, and lasted until the first decades of the 5th century BC.

Painters included the painters of Paris, Anfiarao, Tityos, Silenus, Micali (this last was from the name of the scholar who published some of his pots).

♦ Daunia pottery

These region, which corresponds to today's northern Apulia, was already producing in the Bronze Age a particular type of painted pottery vase known to local tradition as "ollas", small jugs and bowls with geometric decorations and typical modelled appendages also with full relief figures.

57. Typical water bowl of Daunia manufacture. High vertical modelled handle with overpainting. 5th century BC.

58. Large Apulian manufacture red figure "hydria". Rich and colourful decorations with abundant white overpainting, probably burial accessories. 4th-3rd century BC.

59. Ceremonial red figure amphora with mythological figures. 4th-3rd century BC.

◆ *Apulia red figure pottery*

Initially strongly influenced by Attic red figure pottery, this variety underwent a decline in quality after the cessation of imports from Greece. However this type of production found its own original means of expression in baroque decorations with complex mythological scenes full of figures arranged on different levels, with flowing drapery and enlivened with bright colours which were also overpainted.

◆ *Campania red figure pottery*

The principal Campanian cities involved in red figure pottery manufacture are Capua and

73

60. Typical fish plate. 4th-3rd century BC.

Cuma, with high quality artists producing pottery decorated with scenes depicting local myths, burial scenes and scenes featuring Dionysus. One of the most typical types of production from these workshops is the so-called "fish plate".

♦ *Gnatian pottery*

This takes its name from the city of Gnatia but the main production centre was undoubtedly Taranto. It is characterised by thick

61. Small overpainted jug, probably manufactured in Taranto. 4th-3rd century BC.

black shiny paint with decorative elements which include human and animal figures as well as plants.

The shapes are generally suited for tableware with pots of small dimensions, mainly small jugs.

The Albites Collection

The collection of the Marchese Albites di San Paterniano is one of the most outstanding in the whole museum. Various objects were donated to the Museum in several stages between 1878 and 1922, only a few of which came from Fiesole. Most of the items were the result of excavations and searches in the antiques markets, especially in Rome.

The Marchese was a friend of Marchese Carlo Strozzi whom he joined in the Roman theatre excavations, and had tried to establish his own museum which was to be situated in a few ground-floor rooms of what is now the Council building. This attempt was unsuccessful, due in part to the determined opposition of the Head of the Service, Milani,

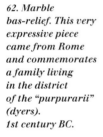

62. Marble bas-relief. This very expressive piece came from Rome and commemorates a family living in the district of the "purpurarii" (dyers). 1st century BC.

63. Apulian red figure "pelike". 4th century BC.

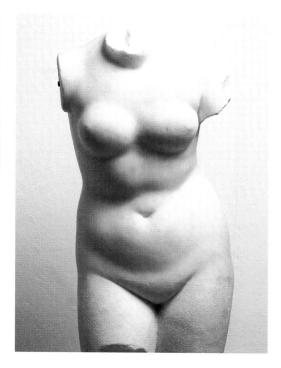

64. Venus rising from the waters. Marble copy of a Greek original. This has recently been restored and is one of the most beautiful pieces in the museum.

who did not approve of the foundation of a new museum with materials from other sources, now that the Archaeological Museum had been established. A great deal of ambiguity also surrounded the authenticity of many of Albites' pieces.

Materials from other Collections

One of the most outstanding collection groups preserved and displayed in the Museum is the collection donated by the Colombaria Society of Florence. This consists of many items of red earth pottery from excavations in the Chiusi and Sovana areas. Other donations were made by figures who in one way or another were prominent in Fiesole society. The first of these is Stefanelli, the first director of the Museum who not only donated a series of interesting iron tools but also convinced others to make donations. Among these were Giorgio Carocci (items from

65. Ariballo-type "lekythos", Campanian red figure pottery. Mid-4th century BC.

66. Pyx "olla". End 7th century BC.

Orvieto, Bolsena and Montefiascone), Temistocle Pampaloni, mayor of Fiesole from 1877-1899, and Anton Domenico Pierrugues.

67. Female head "oinochoe", Attic red figure pottery. 5th century BC.

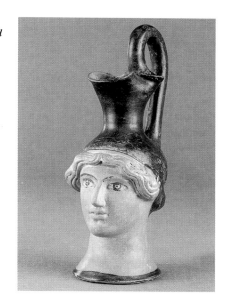

68. Attic red figure "kylix". 5th century BC.

69. Attic black figure "hydria". End 6th century BC.

70. Etruscan-Corinthian "kylix". Second quarter 6th century BC.

Finito di stampare nel mese di aprile 1999
presso Giunti Industrie Grafiche S.p.A.
Stabilimento di Prato